01603/739

1901 Cabw.   ... 11-111R

Sailing Basics: Your Beginners Guide

ISBN-13: 978-1480176201
ISBN-10: 1480176206

Copyright Notice

All Rights Reserved © 2012 Richard Trunam

This book is a work of the author's experience and opinion. This book is licensed for your personal enjoyment only. This book may not be re-sold or given away to other people. If you would like to share this book with another person please purchase an additional copy for each person you share it with. You may not distribute or sell this book or modify it in any way. The editorial arrangement, analysis, and professional commentary are subject to this copyright notice. No portion of this book may be copied, retransmitted, reposted, downloaded, decompiled, reverse engineered, duplicated, or otherwise used without the express written approval of the author, except by reviewers who may quote brief excerpts in connection with a review. The scanning, uploading and distribution of this book via the internet or via any other means without permission of the publisher is illegal and punishable by law. The publisher does not have any control over and does not assume any responsibility for author or third-party websites or their content. United States laws and regulations are public domain and not subject to copyright. Any unauthorized copying, reproduction, translation, or distribution of any part of this material without permission by the author is prohibited and against the law. Disclaimer and Terms of Use: No information contained in this book should be considered as financial, tax, or legal advice. Your reliance upon information and content obtained by you at or through this publication is solely at your own risk. The authors or publishers assume no liability or responsibility for damage or injury to you, other persons, or property arising from any use of any product, information, idea, or instruction contained in the content or services provided to you through this book. Reliance upon information contained in this material is solely at the reader's own risk. The authors have no financial interest in and receive no compensation from manufacturers of products or websites mentioned in this book. Whilst attempts have been made to verify information provided in this publication, neither the author nor the publisher assumes any responsibilities for errors, omissions or contradictory information contained in this book. The author and publisher make no representation or warranties with respect to the accuracy, applicability, fitness, or completeness of the contents of this book. The information contained in this book is strictly for educational purposes. The author and publisher do not warrant the performance, effectiveness or applicability of any information or sites listed or linked to in this book.

SAILING BASICS: YOUR BEGINNERS GUIDE

Richard Trunam

Dedicated to the lucky souls who've been touched by the fun and exhilaration and sheer buzz of sailing...

Contents

1. The History of Sailing
2. Popularity of Sailing
3. The Rules of Sailing
4. Sailboat Buying Guide
5. The Buying Process
6. Balancing Your Sailboat
7. Sail Controls
8. Using a Winch
9. Using the Sail
10. Seeing the Wind
11. Adjusting the Mainsail on Reaches
12. Running Before the Wind
13. Increase Your Sailing Speed
14. Off-Season Goals
15. Maintaining Your Sailboat

The History of Sailing

Although people have been engaged in sailing for transportation purposes since the beginning of time, sailing as a sport is believed to have begun only in the 17th century.

The general view is that the sport of sailing originated in Holland and was then introduced in England in the year 1660 by Charles II.

In the years that followed, the popularity of the sport also spread to America and its colonies.

It was just as common back then as it is today for those engaged in sport sailing to gather for both recreational and social purposes.

The group of people who join in these gatherings are known as yacht clubs.

The world saw the establishment of the very first yacht club at Cork, Ireland in 1720.

In the United States, the oldest known yacht club that continues to exist even to this day is the New York Yacht Club, which was established in 1844.

In the year 1851, NYYC members raced the schooner named America against competitors from Britain.

The race was held around the Isle of Wight in England and was won by the NYYC delegates.

After the victory, the sailors deeded the trophy they had won to the NYYC and it then became known as America's Cup.

This was the same name given to the oldest and what's believed to be the most prestigious international sailboat racing event in existence.

Every single America's Cup event that was held from 1951 was won by the United States until their winning streak was broken by Australia in 1983.

The 1980s and 90s saw some radical changes in the design of the boats used in the sport. These decades also saw espionage charges and sabotage marring the America's Cup competitions.

The United States team won the Cup again in 1987 and then once again lost it in 1995 to New Zealand.

New Zealand was once again adjudged the winner in the year 2000, but lost out to Switzerland in the year 2003.

The America's Cup competitions have seen longer and lighter boats using a higher mast that carry more sail ever since 1992.

Another sport sailing event that has increasingly gained popularity over the years is ocean racing, which is known to be a dangerous and arduous sport, particularly when it involves long-distance solo events.

Among the major events that belong to this category are the Volvo Ocean Race, the Transpacific Race, and the Newport-Bermuda Race.

The Volvo Ocean Race was formerly called Whitbread Round the World Race.

In the year 1967, the world of sailing marked one of its milestones when Francis Chichester successfully circumnavigated the earth with only a single stop.

This resulted in the introduction of the Golden Globe, which is a non-stop, around-the-world solo sailing race first held the year after Chichester's accomplishment.

These days, the boats used by those who participate in the sport of sailing are multi-hulled yachts that are equipped with the latest features technology has to offer.

They have satellite-generated updates on the weather and sophisticated communication equipment.

And sailboat racing has become so popular that's it's even been included in the Olympic Games since 1900. Olympic sailors now compete in a total of nine classes.

But, perhaps the best news is that sailing has evolved from being an exclusive sport for the wealthy to a sport that welcomes much wider participation by the regular folk.

Popularity of Sailing

Sailing is generally considered as an activity that requires a high level of skills. Because of this reputation, it has grown to be one of the most widely-recognized and well-organized sports in the world.

There's a wide variety of sailing events and there are also a number of different categories both for sailing and other boating events.

Some of the popular sailing events revolve around making or breaking world records. There are also those that focused mainly on the act of racing for a pre-determined distance or period of time.

Among the most popular sport sailing events are yacht racing, cruisers, catamarans, speed boating, kite surfing, wind surfing, and model boat racing.

There are plenty of short-distance races being held in protected bodies of water like harbours. Long-distance races, on the other hand, are typically held in the open sea.

The primary purpose for this segregation is to protect marine life in the seas and to keep waterways uninterrupted by the usually large number of boats participating in sailing races.

If you plan to sail for purposes of competition, then you should bear in mind that knowledge and skills are the keys to winning sailing events.

Whether you choose to sail solo, with a partner, or as part of a crew, you'll surely increase your chances of winning by enhancing your sailing knowledge and skills.

Among the most basic knowledge you need to gain is a knowledge of the winds and the different ways of sailing through them.

Such knowledge makes it a lot easier for you to make quick and well-informed decisions as well as to prepare for whatever conditions you'll be facing out on the water.

Your speed will naturally increase when you're able to angle the boat to the wind correctly and achieve an even keel. This knowledge also makes you more capable of determining when you need to trim the sails so as to reduce drag.

If you choose to race on a crewed boat, then you need to realize the value of teamwork and communication. You need to learn how to work well with the other members of the crew so as to achieve balance and prevent losing any time as you watch the currents, the winds, and the proper angling of your boat.

You may even want to consider joining any of the Olympic sailing events once you feel you've gained the necessary level of skills.

Sailing has been an Olympic sport for more than a hundred years and many of those who choose to engage in the sport also dream of becoming an Olympian one day.

At present, the British hold the number one ranking in the sport, closely followed by the Americans.

The popularity of sailing as a serious sport has indeed grown considerably since it was first introduced in the 17th century.

It is no wonder, then, why more and more people have chosen to learn how to sail in recent years.

If you're one of those who plan to sail regularly for the years to come, then you should start increasing your knowledge and skills in the sport as early as now!

The Rules of Sailing

In sailing competitions, there are several boats traversing the same course in the same body of water. This makes it extremely important for you to learn and follow sailing rules.

In fact, if you're sailing on a boat that measures 39.4 feet or more in length, then you're required to have a copy of the rules and regulations on sailing.

And even if you sail on a smaller boat, it's still important for you to have a definite and clear knowledge of these rules in order to ensure the safety of everyone concerned.

When you sail without adequate knowledge of the rules, you're actually putting yourself at risk of being liable for any untoward incident that may occur.

The rules governing the sport of sailing have been crafted based on common sense.

Furthermore, these rules espouse very simple ideas that should leave no doubt whatsoever as regards who is given preference in the event that boats come too close to each other.

Take note that race organizers typically enforce these rules and regulations very strictly.

If you happen to be the stand-on vessel in such a scenario, then you should be prepared to change your course.

If you happen to be on the vessel that's given right-of-way, then you should provide clear directions as regards your intentions, take all the necessary precautions, and then steer your path safely.

In most cases, vessels that broke down and power-driven vessels are given right-of-way.

Another thing you should be knowledgeable in if you hope to be any good at sailing is the function of buoys, which are basically markers that indicate threat such as rocks, shoals, and wrecks.

There are four basic types of buoys and these are:

1. Lateral markers, which indicate channel edges so you can steer safely along.

2. Cardinal buoys that are usually marked black and yellow to indicate dangers to the North, South, East, or West.

3. Dennis the Menace buoys, which are typically black and red, that indicate isolated danger.

4. Safe water buoys that are usually red and white, and indicate safe navigation.

As a beginner in the sport of sailing, you should also be aware of the importance of sound signals as a means of communicating with other vessels.

Following are some general sound signals used in sailing. Take note, though, that international signals could vary.

1. If you plan to turn starboard side, then you should give one short blast so the other boat knows to stay port side.

2. If you plan to turn port side, then you should give two short blasts so the other boat knows to stay on starboard side.

3. If you plan to reverse your engines, then you should give three short blasts.

4. When you're ready to get underway, then you should give one long blast.

5. If you want the other boat to open their drawbridge, then you should give a long blast that's immediately followed by a short blast.

6. If you're in danger and want the other boat to immediately move out of your way, then you should give five short blasts.

If you're "the other boat", then you should know that general rules require you to repeat the signal given to confirm that you understood it.

If you feel that the intended action poses a real danger, then you need to respond with five short blasts.

These are, of course, just a few of the sailing rules you need to learn. The good thing is that it's easy enough to learn the other rules as you go along.

Sailboat Buying Guide

Buying a sailboat involves a lot more self-evaluation than just picking out the very first or the cheapest boat you see.

Among the most important things you need to consider are type, size, and cost.

Other than these considerations, you also have to think about how you'll be using the boat and for what purpose.

The best way to prepare for buying the right sailboat is to ask yourself the following questions:

1. **What type of boat fits you and your needs best?**
   To answer this question, you need to learn about the different types of sailboat. Other than that, you also need to consider where you'll be sailing and whether you'll be day sailing or cruising. Will you be sailing only on weekends or for longer periods of time? Furthermore, you have to decide whether you'll be using your boat for sailing someday.

2. **What size of sailboat do you need?**
   When deciding on the right size of sailboat to get, you need to consider the cost of your

sails, gear, berthing, and winter storage, among other things.

Naturally, maintenance and other expenses are much higher on bigger boats. You should also reflect on whether you'll mostly be sailing solo or with a crew. If cruising is part of your plans, then you should consider how many crew members you'll have on board.

3. **Will a new sailboat be better for you than a used one?**
   Consider the difference between getting the convenience of a brand-new sailboat even at a higher price and saving a considerable amount by buying a used sailboat that can sufficiently address your needs.

   Ask yourself if you have the time and capability for maintaining and upgrading a used boat. Are you a do-it-yourself type of person who enjoys such projects as boat maintenance and repair?

As for the cost considerations you need to make, you may want to take note of the following:

1. **There are plenty of sailboats on sale, particularly at this time when the economy is down**
   Boat owners tend to invest a good deal of money in improving their sailboats, so you're likely to get a whole set of top-quality gear for much less than you'd spend on a new boat. What's important is for you to choose your boat carefully and not rush into things. If a used boat that's being sold requires a lot of repairs and upgrades, then it may eventually cost you much more than a brand-new boat.

2. **Are you capable of renovating and improving a used boat on your own?**
   The costs for boat repairs and upgrades can become quite expensive. This makes it highly beneficial for you to have the skills and the time to do the repairs and upgrading by yourself. You should also be prepared to spend some time shopping for used gear you might need.

3. **Take note of all related costs of making a boat purchase**
   One of the most important and often the highest cost related to a boat purchase is insurance. It may be wise to get estimates beforehand. Berthing costs should also be

taken into consideration. Finally, bear in mind that boat loans generally carry much higher interest rates than mortgages.

Once you've carefully considered all these things, you should be ready to start the actual boat buying process.

The Buying Process

To make sure you get the right boat for your needs, it's best to follow these steps in sailboat shopping:

1. **Take Your Time**
   Beware of falling head-over-heels for the very first boat that seems to meet all of your needs. Acting on impulse by buying that boat could lead to frustration and regret later on.

   What you need to do instead is analyze all the costs involved, decide which type and size of boat you need, and then stick to that plan. Do your homework and search the Internet to get a general idea of how much your chosen type of boat costs.

2. **Get a Full-boat Survey on a Used Boat**
   Hire the services of an accredited marine surveyor, preferably one who specializes in sailboats and is a member of ACMS, NAMS, or SAMS. If you're checking out a larger boat, then it may be a good idea to get a separate survey for its engine.

   If you're checking out an older boat, then you have to be prepared to spend a little more to have the boat pulled out of the water so its hull can be checked.

Remember that foregoing a survey could lead to some very expensive problems later on. Besides, a survey could very well be one of the requirements for securing insurance.

Take note as well that you can use any problem found in a survey as basis for negotiating the boat's price. The savings you get from negotiations is usually more than what you'd spend on the survey.

You should also learn how to inspect the boat yourself, as you'll be doing most of the maintenance work in the future.

3. **Request a Sea Trial**

    You can't really gauge how well a boat sails unless you've been sailing on it. You just might discover that a boat that looked perfect for you doesn't really sail as you expect it to or perhaps doesn't quite match your style.

    You may want to take the survey while you're sailing, since there are certain systems that can only be successfully tested underway.

    A sea trial is also the most effective way of checking the status of a boat's running rig, sails, and other features. Allow the owner to sail the boat and then observe him very carefully. Does he have a tendency to make excuses for the way certain things work or fail to work? Treat that as a warning.

4. Choose Your Boat and Negotiate the Price

If your gut tells you there's just something that isn't quite right with a boat, then don't buy it no matter how lovely it looks. If it does feel perfect, then you should learn what the asking prices for similar boats are so you'll know where to start negotiating.

Used boats are almost always flexible in their price, since there's usually something that needs to be repaired or upgraded. Remember that the time of year can also work to your advantage.

If you're shopping for a boat towards the end of the season, then you'll have a much better chance of lowering the price of the boat.

The owner will likely prefer passing on the problem of storage to you and will therefore be more willing to accept a much lower amount.

Perhaps the most important thing you need to remember when you're shopping for a sailboat is that if you have any questions at all, you should never hesitate to ask.

Balancing Your Sailboat

If you truly want to learn how to sail competitively, then you need to learn how to practice the art and science of balance. Have you ever watched those Kung Fu movies wherein the master tells his student about yin and yang?

Well, you'll have to rediscover these same secrets of balance if you want to gain the ability to sail much faster and more powerfully than before.

To start with, you need to see your sailboat as a large wind vane, similar to what you usually see on the roof of a barn. This vane usually consists of a long shaft with an arrow at one end and some sort of figure at the other end.

Now, let's convert these parts of a weather vane into a sailboat. The long shaft shall represent your sailboat hull, from the bow to the stern.

The arrow will then represent the bow of your sailboat and the figure on the other end will represent your mainsail, since it has the largest surface area.

Take note that as the breeze picks up, a weather vane normally turns such that the arrow is facing the wind and the figure is set farthest from the wind. The wind therefore blows directly against the figure, since it has the largest surface area.

Getting back to your sailboat, you therefore need to hoist your mainsail up the mast so that most of its surface is exposed to the wind at the boat's far side.

When you let go of your sailboat's tiller or wheel, you'll notice that it'll naturally want to pivot the bow into the wind the way the weather vane turns the arrow to face the wind.

How, then, can you achieve balance in your sailboat such that she practically steers herself?

Well, you could poistion other sails right near the bow. When there's light to moderate wind, you could use a larger headsail.

Always remember that sails are basically soft foils, but sailcloth has a tendency to change its shape due to the strength of the wind.

Mainsails are typically created with their draft at about 45-55 percent aft of the luff whereas Genoa sails are made with their draft at about 30-40 percent aft of the luff. Your primary objective as you sail is to keep the draft at their original locations.

Take note that the draft is likely to creep farther aft as the wind grows stronger.

You should therefore move it back into the right position using tension. Use the halyard to create tension and sight up the sail so the draft can move back into position.

When you finally understand the secrets of balance where sailboats are concerned, then you can truly start learning how to sail just like the pros.

Take heed of the sailing tips above to increase your balancing skills and your confidence in your ability to sail wherever you may choose to bring your boat.

Once you've mastered the basics of balancing your sailboat, you'll have to bring your skills a step higher by learning to gain balance even in heavy and gusty winds.

Sail Controls

When you gain a better understanding of the basic controls of your sailboat, you'll surely learn how to sail faster.

Following are some of the most important sailing terms you need to learn if you ever hope to understand how to manipulate the controls on your boat.

Remember that these controls serve as the gears and throttles of your sailboat. To begin with, your boat's mainsail is typically controlled from the boom and mast.

Here are the controls most often used by a sailing crew:

1. **The Mainsheet**
   You need to be able to control your sailboat's boom and that's exactly what the mainsheet can do. It is comprised of pulleys attached to the middles or end of the deck and boom.

   Easing the mainsheet lets the boom swing away from your boat while trimming it brings the boom closer.

2. **The Traveller**
   This thin, flat bar, which is installed from one side to the other, aids in adjusting the boom's position.

3. **The Traveller Car**
   Most mainsheets have a bottom block that's attached to a device known as a mainsheet car. This slides along the traveller to give you more control over the mainsail.

Your headsail will need to have lines and winches so you can keep control over it and make the necessary adjustments to shape it for optimum performance.

Here are the control devices for your headsail:

1. **Genoa Sheet**
   Each headsail on a boat has two sheets or control lines that attach to the sail's clew.

2. **Lead Block**
   Once the headsail's sheets are attached, lead each of them along the boat's side and then thread them through the lead block. This block serves to direct the line right back to the boat's cockpit sheet winch.

3. **Sheet Winch**
   Each of the headsail's sheets goes from the block to a winch on each side. The loads on a Genoa that's filled with wind are typically very high, which is why you'll need a winch to provide you with mechanical advantage for pulling in on the Genoa sheet. Be sure to take at least three clockwise wraps on your winch before grinding it.

Take note that there are also controls common to both the mainsail and the headsail. These controls include the following:

1. **Halyards**
   Each sail is hoisted using the halyard, the end of which has a shackle attached to the sail's head. You'll need to raise the sail right to topmast before tying it off.

2. **Halyard Winch**
   Each halyard also has a winch of its own, which allows you to put enough tension on the luff so as to shape the sail. Again, be sure to take at least three clockwise wraps before grinding the winch.

3. **Winch Handle**
   The end of a winch handle is typically ratchet-shaped and fits right into the centre of the drum. Make sure it's long enough for you to grind without making too much effort. It's best to stow it in a handle pocket or in the cockpit so you don't lose it.

4. **Boom Vang**
   Whenever the end of the boom goes beyond the side of the sailboat, the mainsheet will lack the necessary "umph" for pulling down on the mainsail's leech. This is where you need a boom vang. This simple block and tackle attaches to the underside of the mast and then to the bottom of the boom.

So now you know the basics on sail controls. You should be ready to increase your speed and power when you go sailing.

You'd also do well to increase your knowledge on the different ways to steer a sailboat.

Using a Winch

You'll surely be able to sail with more confidence when you've learned how to use a sailboat's winches.

These devices can effectively reduce the time and effort needed for trimming sails so as to achieve more power and speed.

Let's say, for example, that a heavy breeze makes it necessary for you to trim the sail. As you grab the line and pull, it could become almost impossible for you to hold due to the tension that the wind creates. This is where the sailboat winch enters the picture. These mechanical devices are shaped like an hourglass. Its middle part is known as a drum and contains gears inside.

In conjunction with the winch handle, these gears increase the ability of the winch to keep you from having to engage in back-breaking work.

Here are the steps you need to follow so as to ensure safe sail trimming:

1. **Lead the Line-in Up to the Winch**
   Make sure the line you plan to take to the winch actually leads up to it. On some boats,

you may notice the line leading down and that could be a bit dangerous.

The lead of a line may be changed with the use of a block, which can help you point the line towards the correct direction.

Lead blocks should be positioned between the winch and sail clew such that the sail sheet leads up the winch at an angle. Make sure the block is kept a little lower than the drum to ensure the sail sheet is always at an upward angle to the drum.

2. Wrap the Sheet Clockwise

Pull the sheet towards the winch and then turn it clockwise around the drum. The full turn you make is called a wrap.

Make sure that every successive wrap you make is parallel to the one preceding it and held flat against the drum. Wraps shouldn't be stacked on top of each other, as that can cause jammed turns that freeze the wraps onto the drum.

3. Count Your Wraps

If you're sailing on a small boat, remove the slack from the sail sheet by wrapping once around the drum and then make one or two more wraps to hold the sail sheet in place. If you're sailing on a larger boat, you'll need to make three to four more wraps to hold the sail sheet in place. If you have a thinner line, then you'll have to make even more wraps.

You'll then need to hold these wraps in place by pulling on the line with a bit of tension. This is called tailing and it keeps the wraps properly aligned on the drum.

There are winches equipped with two clamshell plates into which you should jam the line after completing the wraps so as to hold it in place.

4. **Grind the Winch**
   Turn the winch drum to trim the sail. This effectively pulls in the halyard or sheet so you can properly shape the sails for power or speed. Place a winch handle into the hole in the centre of the drum's top plate.

   Hover over the winch while keeping your back straight. Hold the line or sheet with one hand and then turn the handle with the other. Remove the handle when you're done grinding and then cleat off the line.

5. **Cast or Ease Off**
   Ease the sheet with your dominant hand. Remove it from the cleat or in the case of a self-tailing winch, remove the wrap from the clam plates. Use moderate tension to hold the line and wraps in place. Use moderate pressure in holding the wraps with the palm of your non-dominant hand.

   Ease the sail sheet an inch or two with a smooth motion and then brake. Repeat the ease-brake motion. When there's a need for lowering a sail or changing tacks, you'll have to cast-off the line.

As long as you keep the above tips in mind when you sail, you should be able to sail safely and with a lot more confidence than before.

Using the Sail

If you truly want to sail like the pros, then you'll have to learn one of the sport's most useful and fun exercises – that is, sailing without rudders.

Take note that a boat's rudder is vulnerable to underwater obstruction of all kinds. And while tillers have very few moving parts, its rudder post could get jammed, thus keeping the rudder itself pulled to one side.

On the other hand, a sailboat wheel is comprised of several wires and pulleys that turn the rudder any way you want.

When even just one of these components fail, you're likely to lose your rudder. This is why it's important for you to learn how to use the sail and your crew weight in steering the boat.

If you're sailing on a smaller sailboat, crew weight can be very effective for turning your boat either downwind or upwind.

Let's assume that you're out on the water during a particularly windy day and you have two crew members sailing with you. if you want the bow of your boat to turn downwind, then you need to get all crew members into the cockpit, thus shifting a large part of the weight astern. This will make the boat's stern sink lower and focus the force of the wind on the bow as it rises.

Now, if you want the bow to turn upwind, you simply have to do the opposite. Shift crew weight near the bow to make it sink lower and focus the force of the wind on the stern.

When you're sailing on a larger boat, you may add weight by moving anchors and anchor chains along with your crew weight.

Your sails can also be used in the same way you use the weight of your crew. Bear in mind that the force of the wind will always focus on the part of your sailboat that has the largest surface area.

If you want the bow of your boat to turn upwind, then you should raise only the mainsail, which is located near the stern. The force of the wind will therefore cause the stern to turn downwind.

If, however, you want the bow to turn downwind, you need to lower your mainsail and raise the Genoa. The Genoa is located near the bow, so the force of the wind will effectively turn the bow downwind.

Now that you've gained a better understanding of how to steer a sailboat using only crew weight and the sails, it's time to put this knowledge into practice.

Follow these steps to experience the thrill and adventure of one of the most vital sailing skills:

1. Find a location where you'll have plenty of room to practice until you get the hang of steering by crew weight and sails.

2. Raise the mainsail and the Genoa and then balance the sailboat for the existing wave and wind conditions. Whenever necessary, reduce headsail and reef the mainsail. Position your boat such that you can easily sail with a light pressure of your fingertips on the tiller or wheel.

3. Pick a particular point you'll be sailing to that's about a mile or two away.

4. Assign one of your crew members to work the mainsail and the other to work the Genoa.

5. Sail in a straight line towards your chosen destination.

These basic techniques will definitely go a long way towards helping you sail like the pros. Now you can go out on the water with or without a rudder.

… Seeing the Wind

If you're like most people, then it may be a little difficult for you to visualize exactly where the wind is coming from when you first start learning how to sail.

Perhaps you've decided to make use of sail telltales, which are short pieces of ribbon or yarn attached to the edge of the sail.

There is, however, a more effective way for you to become a better and more independent sailor. Once you learn how to see the wind, you'll definitely be more in tune with it and with the waves.

There are sailors who "see" the wind by feeling the way it touches their cheeks, their ears, and even their napes.

They're able to develop this skill such that they can successfully sail even with their eyes closed.

In fact, you'd be amazed to know that there are international sailing races held among blind sailors and many of these sailors have successfully sailed across thousands of miles of the sea.

With the right amount of practice, you can train yourself to see the wind in this manner as well.

The good thing is that this will increase your speed and confidence while enhancing your performance as well.

Perhaps the best news is that you don't even need to be on a sailboat in order to practice.

Here's a simple exercise that can get you started in developing the ability to see the wind when you sail:

1. Go outside when there's a good breeze.

2. Identify an area that's free from obstructions.

3. Relax, clear your mind, and focus on feeling the wind.

4. Turn your body such that you're facing the wind.

5. Close your eyes and try to block out as much of the sunlight as possible by putting on a pair of sunglasses.

6. Focus on the wind and keep adjusting your body until you truly feel that you're square to the wind.

7. Turn your body to the right a little and keep turning until you finally feel the wind against your left cheek and ear. Make sure your body is aligned 90 degrees to the direction of the wind.

8. Continue rotating slowly to the right until you've got your back to the wind. Observe closely how the wind feels against your nape.

9. Continue rotating slowly to the right and then stop when the wind blows against your right cheek and ear. In the same way you did with your left cheek, adjust your position such that your body is at a 990-degree angle to the direction of the wind and then continue turning until you're square into the wind.

10. Open your eyes and relax. Do the exercise again, this time rotating to the left. Remember to stop for a few minutes at every position described above.

Keep practicing this exercise several times each week until the ability to "see" the wind becomes second nature. This ability will surely make you a more confident and better-skilled sailor, regardless of where you choose to sail.

Adjusting the Mainsail on Reaches

If you truly want to gain the ability to sail well, then you'll have to learn how to adjust a boat's mainsail every time you reach a point of sail.

This section provides you with some useful tips on how to do just that. The points of sail where you're not beating or running are known as reaches.

Being the fastest of all points of sail, reaches can be a lot of fun. If you want to sail well on reaches, you'll need to start purely with the mainsail.

It's best to shape your mainsail by using both the mainsheet and the boom vang. The mainsheet is typically located near the helm and helps keep the trailing edge of the mainsail under control.

It also gives you control over the boom's horizontal position in relation to the centreline of the sailboat.

The centreline is an imaginary line going down the middle of the sailboat from the bow to the stern. The boom vang aids in keeping the boom horizontal when you sail onto reaches.

Since the end of the boom is no longer over the sailboat, the mainsheet will no longer be able to pull down on it. The boom vang then does the mainsheet's job at this point. Here are a few easy exercises you can practice so as to learn how to trim the mainsail on reaches:

1. **Hoist the mainsail**
   When sailing onto a reach, remember to put just enough tension on the boom vang to keep the boom horizontal. Allowing an inch or two of give will usually prevent problems.

2. **Sail onto a close reach**
   This is the first point of sail where you'll no longer be beating. You need to set the boom such that the end is aligned with the edge of the boat.

   Choose a specific point in the distance and then make sure the bow is always pointed in that direction. Check the wind indicator at the top of the mast. Note how the arrow orients to the V just below it.

3. **Fall farther off-wind to a beam reach**
   Ease the boom out somewhere about halfway between the shrouds and the centreline. Orient the bow at a 90-degree angle to the true wind.

It's best to make use of anchored boats, wind waves, or flags to help you accomplish this. Once again, you need to choose a distant point that'll help you steer.

4. **Fall farther off-wind to a broad reach**
   Ease the boom out to a point about three-quarters between the shrouds and the centreline. Orient the sailboat with the wind behind the boat's beam.

   Again, you should choose a point in the distance and then steer in that direction.

5. **Turn the sailboat towards the wind to a beam reach**
   Do the same thing you did in Step 3 and then repeat Step 2. Keep practicing this sequence until you familiarize all points of reaching.

By practicing these steps, you should be able to successfully improve your sailing skills. It won't be long until you master sailing just like a pro!

Running Before the Wind

You can continue improving your sailing skills until you're ready to turn pro and among the things you need to learn along the way is the ability to run before the wind.

This means you sail with the wind blowing over your sailboat's stern.

Perhaps the best thing about this is that it is the most relaxing point of sail.

But, relaxing though it may be, this still requires a good deal of concentration from you so as to avoid what's known as a flying jibe.

This is when your sailboat's boom swings from one side to the other.

Here are a number of very simple steps you can take to practice running before the wind in a safe way:

1. Ask a sailing buddy to help you get your sailboat underway. Find an open area that doesn't have a lot of traffic, shallow water, or buoys so you can practice in peace and safety.

2. Attach a 9-inch piece of yarn in any dark colour to each of the upper shrouds. Shrouds

are the longest wires found on the side of a sailboat. These shroud telltales will help you "see" the wind, particularly if you still haven't mastered that art.

3. Raise the mainsail only. You can move on to using a jib, a Genoa, or a colourful spinnaker with your mainsail to gain more speed once you've mastered the skill of running before the wind by controlling only the mainsail.

4. Fall off towards the right of the wind's direction. This should place you onto port track. Be sure to do this just a little at a time and in a smooth and slow motion. As you slowly fall off the wind, let out your mainsheet.

5. Observe the shroud telltale on the left. Notice that the more you fall off, the more it points towards the sailboat's bow.

6. The moment the left shroud telltale appears to point a little bit towards starboard, you should stop the boat. Choose an object or a point of land straight ahead of the boat's bow and then use that as a reference point for steering.

7. Check the left shroud telltale from time to time to ensure it's still pointing towards the right side of your sailboat's bow.

    Adjust your steering so as to keep this alignment and continue to run before the wind until such time that you run out of sailing room. Head up to a close-hauled course or sail onto a reach so can stay in safe waters.

You can follow a similar set of steps when sailing on starboard tack. In that case, however, you'll have to use the right shroud telltale.

Keep the telltale aligned such that it points towards the left of the sailboat's bow.

If, at any point, you notice that the boom is about to swing into a flying jibe, always bear this in mind: "Tiller Toward, Wheel Away."

This means if you're using a tiller, then you need to push it towards the boom.

However, if you're sailing with a wheel, then you need to turn it away from the boom.

Remember to move the tiller or wheel just enough to gain control and then follow the above steps once again.

Increase Your Sailing Speed

Would you like to experience sailing with more speed when you're beating to windward?

If so, then you'll definitely want to learn the following three strategies for enhancing windward sailing performance:

1. **Setting Sail Shape for Pointing**
   You need to trim your sails to achieve the best windward shape. Pull in the mainsheet such that the boom lies near the centreline.

   Look up the sail's trailing edge. It should reflect a little twist halfway up the sail.

   Look at the topmost batten. It should be parallel to the boat's boom when there's moderate air. When there's super-light air, it should cock a few degrees to leeward. When there's heavy air, the mainsheet car should be slid leeward and the mainsheet eased so there's more twist in the mainsail's upper part.

   Set the jib such that the leech is positioned two to three inches off of the spreaders' tips.

   Achieve a more powerful shape in light air by moving the headsail sheet block forward a bit.

2. **Learning to Use Footing to Sail in Light Air**

   When you sail in super-light air, you'll generally be unable to point as high as you may like. Most sailboats point at their best when the wind reaches at least six knots.

   Anything less will likely cause a loss of pointing ability, which eventually leads to slower sailing. This is where you can take advantage of the art known as footing. This involves building up speed by falling off to a close reach.

   Once you've achieved acceleration, you need to return to sailing close hauled. When you start losing speed again, just repeat the process to maximize your momentum.

3. **Using the Shoreline to Check Your Progress**

   Every time you adjust the sail trim, you need to check your progress using a reference point. Although you can take advantage of a speed-measuring device, you should always use your eyes when you're sailing near land.

   Watch the movement of an object on the shoreline relative to your sailboat. When there's super-light air, you may watch the bubbles behind your boat. These references should let you know at a glance whether your adjustment increased or reduced the boat's speed.

If you happen to lose speed, try half of the sail trim adjustment you just made.

For example, if you just pulled the boom in six inches, then you should try letting it out three inches and then check your reference point again. You'll be surprised at how much difference an inch or two can make as regards speed and performance.

By taking heed of these little-known sailing tips, you'll definitely see marked improvements in your sailing skills.

Who knows, you may even start beating the competition in a race!

It is indeed advisable to learn some new strategies and techniques that may not be very popular with other sailors, but may actually help you bring your sailing performance to the next level.

Striving to constantly improve your skills is still the best way to sail towards becoming a pro.

Off-Season Goals

Have you started learning how to sail but then put off further training until the next season?

Well, if you really want to sail like the pros someday, then you'll have to set goals for yourself even in the off-season.

Yes, indeed there are a number of things you can do to improve your sailing skills even without having to go out on the water.

You can increase your knowledge about the sport, for one thing.

Take note that having more knowledge allows you to enhance your skills a lot faster than ever.

Here are three goals you'd do well to achieve during the off-season:

1. **Learn a New Sailing Term Each Day**
   Sailing season typically begins as the spring season arrives. You can spend the months before that in learning new sailing terms to equip you for the arrival of the new season.

   Although sailing terms can easily be learned, you'll have to repeat them to yourself over and over again until they come naturally to you. As long as you take the time to learn one sailing term each day in the off-season, you should be ready to "talk sailing" like a pro by the time sailing season finally arrives.

2. **Join a Sailing Forum**
   Gain more knowledge and find some useful tips in online sailing forums. Such forums typically have topics related to sailboats, seamanship, knot tying, exotic places to visit, and sailboat engines, among other things.

   Perhaps the best thing about these forums is that the folks who frequent them are usually very friendly and willing to assist you in enhancing your sailing skills.

   Of course, they won't be able to help you with your concerns unless you ask.

   So, don't be like other people who simply scan these forums and never take the time to ask.

   Instead, asking at least one question each week on any of these forums should be one of your off-season goals. You'll be surprised at how much the knowledge you get can improve your sailing experience.

3. **Read One Book on Sailing Each Month**
   Visit your local library and ask the librarian where the sailing books are kept.

   Check the shelves and strive to finish at least one book each month. If you're a fast reader, then it would be even better if you could read one book each week!

   The local library can be a treasure chest of sailing books that provide you with the best sailing advice from the pros. And the best thing is that you get to read these books for free!

   Bear in mind that your taxes are used to pay for these libraries, so it's only fitting that you make use of them. This is like taking sailing lessons from the old masters of the sport at no cost whatsoever.

So, you see, you really don't have to spend the off-season completely away from sailing.

You can continue working on improving your performance in the sport simply by achieving the three goals described above.

When sailing season finally arrives, you'll be a lot more confident and probably a much better sailor overall.

Maintaining Your Sailboat

If you're serious about participating in the sport of sailing, then you shouldn't just learn how to sail; you'll have to learn how to take care of your boat as well.

One very important thing you need to learn as regards sailboat maintenance is that the more time you spend on it today, the less you'll have to spend tomorrow.

This is true of deck maintenance, hull maintenance, and rigging maintenance.

Here are a few tips on how to properly maintain your sailboat:

1. **Protect the Docking and Anchor Line**
   A line attached to a sailboat is typically led into a cleat, a piling, a bollard, a ring, a rail, and a sail. It's understandable that the line is bound to get worn somewhere.

   Lengthen the life of your lines by wrapping rags, strips of canvas, or an old garden hose around your docking or anchor line at every point where it passes through a fitting or touches the hull.

2. **Replace Worn Running Rigging Immediately**
   The furling line is the rope that most often gets chafed and worn. Unfortunately, it is also the one that's almost always taken for granted.

   Be sure to check this line on a regular basis and then move on to checking the halyards, main sheets, boom vang, traveller lines, and Genoa sheets for any signs of wear and tear. If any of these lines have gone past its service life, then you'd do well to replace it at once.

3. **Check the Anchor Gear before Sailing**
   The boat anchor is too often taken for granted. It's usually stored at the bow or even inside a locker. Bear in mind the importance of the anchor being ready for use at any time.

   After all, you never know when you'll need to stop in an emergency or use the anchor to keep your boat from being blown right into a lee shore. Be sure to check for any warping on the anchor's shank before going out to sail. Check for signs of wear on all joints of the anchor as well.

4. **Check for Loose or Missing Rigging Pins**
   Stays and shrouds serve to keep the mast in place, provided that they maintain their integrity. You'll have to check every single cotter pin and replace any worn, missing, or broken pin before you set sail.

5. **Stop Leaks While They're Still Small**
   Check out all areas where water could possibly collect. Check sail lockers, cabin lockers, engine drip pans, bilges, and the anchor well.

   You'll also have to check the shaft exit if your sailboat has an inboard diesel engine, as this is a notorious leaker along with couplings.

   Take note that leaking in these areas is considered among the major causes of sailboat sinking. It therefore pays to check these areas both before and after you sail.

As long as you keep these tips in mind and follow them, you'll surely be able to save a considerable amount you'd otherwise spend on repairs or a replacement.

Wherever you choose to go sailing and whatever sport sailing events you choose to join, it definitely pays to have a well-maintained sailboat.